Better Homes and Gardens®

Scrapbooking for girls only

Meredith® Books
Des Moines, Iowa

Scrapbooking For Girls Only
Editor: Carol Field Dahlstrom
Writer and Project Designer: Susan M. Banker
Designer: Lyne Neymeyer
Copy Chief: Terri Fredrickson
Copy and Production Editor: Victoria Forlini
Editorial Operations Manager: Karen Schirm
Managers, Book Production: Pam Kvitne, Marjorie J. Schenkelberg, Rick von Holdt, Mark Weaver
Contributing Copy Editor: Margaret Smith
Contributing Proofreaders: Sara Henderson, Jessica Kearney Heidgerken, Karen Schmidt
Photographers: Meredith Photo Studio
Technical Illustrator: Chris Neubauer Graphics, Inc.
Editorial and Design Assistants: Kaye Chabot, Mary Lee Gavin, Karen McFadden
Project Designers: Amanda Johnson, Ashley Johnson, Aimee Kempf, Bailey Petersma, Janet Petersma, Diane Reams, Jana Reams, Jill Reams, Alice Wetzel, Annie Wetzel, Emma Wetzel, Sharon Widdop

Meredith® Books
Editor in Chief: Linda Raglan Cunningham
Design Director: Matt Strelecki
Executive Editor, Food and Crafts: Jennifer Dorland Darling

Publisher: James D. Blume
Executive Director, Marketing: Jeffrey Myers
Executive Director, New Business Development: Todd M. Davis
Executive Director, Sales: Ken Zagor
Director, Operations: George A. Susral
Director, Production: Douglas M. Johnston
Business Director: Jim Leonard

Vice President and General Manager: Douglas J. Guendel

Better Homes and Gardens® Magazine
Editor in Chief: Karol DeWulf Nickell

Meredith Publishing Group
President, Publishing Group: Stephen M. Lacy
Vice President-Publishing Director: Bob Mate

Meredith Corporation
Chairman and Chief Executive Officer: William T. Kerr

In Memoriam: E.T. Meredith III (1933-2003)

All of us at Meredith® Books are dedicated to providing you with information and ideas to create beautiful and useful projects. We welcome your comments and suggestions. Write to us at: Meredith Books, Crafts Editorial Department, 1716 Locust Street—LN112, Des Moines, IA 50309-3023.

If you would like to purchase any of our crafts, cooking, gardening, home improvement, or home decorating and design books, check wherever quality books are sold. Or visit us at: bhgbooks.com

Cover Photograph: Andy Lyons Cameraworks

Find Those Pictures!

Let's face it...you have lots of pictures. You collect pictures of your family, your friends, your pets, and of course yourself—looking totally awesome. You treasure pictures of your soccer team, your school dance, your new clarinet, and even your vacation at the beach. You probably have pictures of your friends taped to your walls, a picture of your favorite guy hidden under your pillow, and a bottom dresser drawer filled with pictures of that camping trip last year. Yes, it's time—time to find, look at (and laugh at), those stacks of photos and put them in your own scrapbook created just by you!

In this book of ideas, you'll find ways to cut, crop, and create the coolest scrapbook ever. You'll find hints for ways to put your pictures on a page and how to write about them so you'll never forget the fun you've had. So grab your pictures from wherever they are and start having some fun—scrapbooking!

Carol Field Dahlstrom

Table of Contents

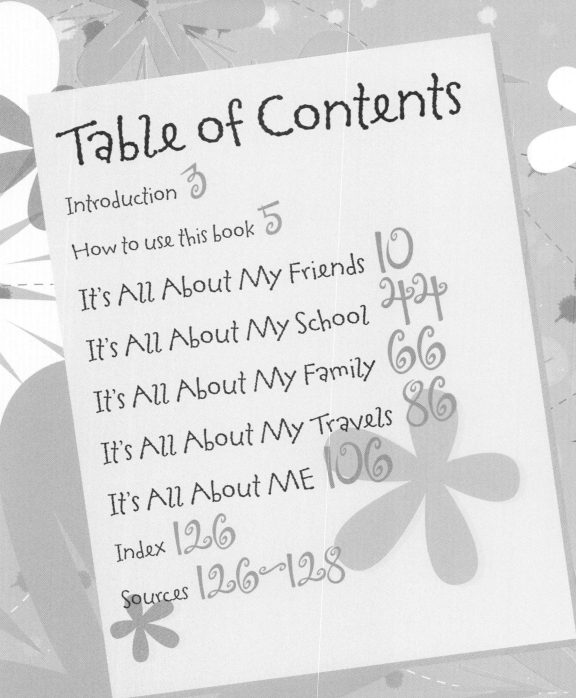

How to use this book

You make a scrapbook because...

making scrapbooking pages is a wonderful way to keep the memories that are so important to you. Scrapbooks combine photos and journaling (writing) that record the highlights of a special day or event. You can make a scrapbook page for any kind of theme—school, friends, family—whatever matters most to you.

This book helps by...

giving you great ideas for scrapbook pages that are geared to all the things GIRLS love! You'll find awesome page samples (that you can re-create step-by-step with your own personal style) grouped in the following chapters:

- It's All About My Friends
- It's All About My School
- It's All About My Family
- It's All About My Travels
- It's All About ME

Whatever matters most to you, you're sure to find tons of inspiration throughout the book!

To get you started...

every scrapbook page in this book starts off with a complete supplies list. To make gathering the stuff easy, we've grouped items in this order:

- Photos (pick out your BEST and most important ones)
- Papers (there are so many cool choices in scrapbooking stores)
- Trims (you'll want to spend your whole allowance on these neat things)
- Tools (basics, such as scissors, paper trimmers, pencils, etc.)
- Computer and printer (if you have these, journaling and headlines willl look oh-so professional)
- Adhesives (glue sticks WILL be your best friend, however, adhesive spacers, double-stick tape, and other glues are fun to use too)

Once you have all the supplies at your work space, you'll find out how to make the page one step at a time. We've even labeled the scrapbook page with numbers to call your attention to specific details. For example, see the circled numbers 1–5 on pages 12–13. It makes following the directions super-simple!

And if you're up for a challenge...

check out the tip boxes sprinkled throughout the book. You'll get even more wonderful ideas that will make your scrapbook pages sparkle with creativity! (Before you know it, your family and friends will be wanting your advice on making pages!)

To get you familiar with the lingo...

The following pages are filled with descriptions of scrapbooking terms (yep, a glossary!) so you can become familiar with them.

Read over the following four pages and then dive right in! You'll find hundreds of fun ideas for scrapbook pages that will have you begging your mom to head to the scrapbook store for supplies. The hardest thing about scrapbooking? Deciding which page to make first!

Have fun creating each page, and thanks for letting us share these ideas for girls with a creative, cool girl like YOU!

Scrapbooking glossary

Acid-free

Acid-free materials help keep photographs and other items on your scrapbook pages from deteriorating. You can buy acid-free paper, glue, pens, scrapbook albums—just about everything. Check the product label if this is important to you.

Adhesive

Scrapbooking adhesives include a glue stick, double-stick tape, spray adhesive, thick white crafts glue, mounting tabs, and other products. Read the labels to find the best adhesive for your use.

Archival quality

"Archival quality" is a term used to label materials that have undergone laboratory tests to show that their acidic and buffered content is within safe levels. (Let's just say, they'll last for a long, long time!)

Borders

Precut strips of patterned or solid paper used to add decorative edges to a scrapbook page.

Card stock

This heavier-weight paper is often used for the base or background. Card stock has a smooth surface.

Circle cutter

A tool used to cut circles from paper; a circle cutter has an arm with a blade in it that moves around a center bar. Use a circle cutter with a protective mat or glass so the work surface isn't scratched.

Corner rounder

Used like a paper punch, this tool rounds the corners of a photograph or paper.

Crafts knife

Commonly known as an X-Acto knife, this tool has a small blade for cutting paper and other materials. (Ask for adult help—these tools are sharp!)

Cropping

Cutting or trimming a photograph to keep only the most important parts of the image.

Decorative-edge scissors

Available in a wide assortment of cutting blades, these scissors

Adhesives

Album and protective sleeves

Card stock

cut paper and other thin materials with wavy, scalloped, zigzagged, or other decorative edges.

Die cut

A paper cutout in which the *background* is cut away. Die cuts come in hundreds of shapes.

Glossy

A smooth, shiny appearance or finish.

Glue stick

A *solid stick-type glue* that is applied by rubbing.

Journaling

Journaling refers to writing on a *scrapbook page* to tell about the photographs. Journaling can *be done* in your handwriting, with adhesive letters, rub-ons, stencils, or it can *be* done on a computer.

Layout

The arrangement of items on a page. (See page 9 for ideas!)

Marking pens

These felt-tip writing tools are available in a variety of colors and tip widths. Some write on photos.

Mat

Varying weights of paper used to frame photographs using single or multiple layers.

Matte

A dull surface or finish, not shiny or glossy.

Mount

To place one paper on top of another.

Opaque

Colors that are dense and cannot *be seen through*.

Paper cutter

This tool has a surface for holding the paper and a sharp blade that cuts the paper in a straight line. (Ask an adult to help—because these are super-sharp, and some blades are heavy!)

Paper punch

Available in different sizes, these handheld tools punch out circles, hearts, diamonds, and other designs in stencil form.

Corner rounder and paper punch

Decorative-edge scissors

Die cuts

File for organizing papers and pages

Marking pens

Book of precut mat papers

Paper cutter

Scissors

Photo-safe

Photo-safe is a term similar to "archival quality," but used when describing photographs. If it is acid-free then it can be labeled photo-safe.

Protective sleeves

Sleeves are made of plastic and slip over a finished album page. These can be side-loading or top-loading and fit 8½×11 or 12-inch-square pages. Choose only acid-free sleeves if you want your pages to last forever. Vinyl sleeves, usually used for office purposes, are not archival quality and should not be included in your album if you're using acid-free materials.

Rubber stamping

Designs are etched into a rubber mat that is applied to a wood block. This rubber design is inked and pressed to paper or other surfaces to transfer the design. (Don't forget to cover your work surface; the inks can stain!)

Scrapbooking papers

Scrapbooking papers are usually 8½×11-inch rectangles or 12-inch squares. These include solids, patterns, textures, and vellum. (There are thousands of awesome papers out there, and you'll want them all!)

Sepia

A brown tone, usually associated with photographs, that has a warm, antique look.

Stencil

Made from heavy paper or plastic, a stencil is laid flat on a surface, and paint or other medium is applied through the openings of the design to transfer it.

Stickers

Available in plastic, paper, vinyl, fabric, and other materials, stickers can be peeled from a backing paper and pressed into place. (Keep yours organized and protected in a portable file!)

Tracing paper

A sheer sheet of paper that can be seen through, it is usually used to trace a pattern.

Vellum

Available in white, colors, and patterns, this translucent paper has a frosted appearance.

Here are layouts you can try...

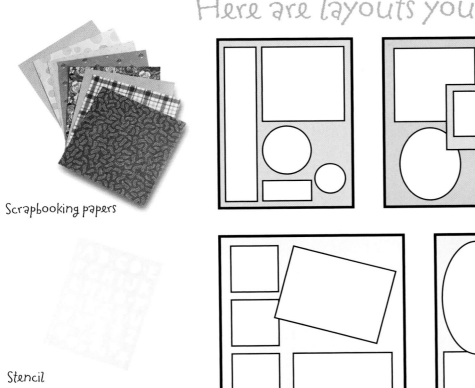

Scrapbooking papers

Stencil

Stickers

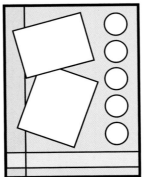

It's All About

My friends

Best Friends

What you'll need

Photos; ruler

Two 12-inch squares of white card stock

Two 11½-inch squares of pink scrapbook paper

Two 10×6-inch pieces of blue scrapbook paper

Two 4×5-inch pieces of blue check paper

Scrapbook papers in white and dark pink

Stickers with friendship, flower, heart, and spiral motifs; marking pen

Scissors; oval template

Computer and printer

Pencil; glue stick

Here's how

Crop around the photos you like, cutting rectangles and an oval shape. To cut the oval, trace around the template on the photo and cut out. Mount the photos on white or dark

Friends share everything from secrets to life's most exciting moments, and these pages capture that very special bond.

Friendship Never Ends

2002-2003
school year

forever friends

pink paper. Trim narrow or wide borders for sticker titles.

1 Glue each large square of pink paper in the center of a sheet of white card stock. Glue the blue papers on the background, ½ inch from the center of the spread, one even with the bottom of the background page and the other even with the top.

2 On the left page, glue the check paper at the top of the blue band. On the right page, glue the check paper in the lower right-hand corner.

3 Using a computer, print the journaling on white paper. Cut out the journal box and glue to dark pink paper.

4 Stick friendship and decorative stickers to wide mats on white paper. Glue to dark pink paper, creating a border.

5 Draw a dotted line around each white paper rectangle using a marking pen. Glue items on the pages. Add stickers where you wish.

You've Gotta Have Friends

What you need

- Photos; ruler
- Two 12-inch squares print background papers
- Coordinating scrapbook papers
- Solid paper triangles, such as Creative Memories
- Beaded wire words, such as "laugh" and "dream," from company such as Wire Expressions
- Flower stickers
- Friendship-theme stickers
- Acrylic jewels
- Dragonfly stencil
- Seed beads
- Fine-line marking pen
- Decorative-edge scissors
- Paper trimmer
- Templates for ovals and circles
- Decorative corner rounder
- Thick white crafts glue
- Glue stick

You and your girlfriends will love looking at pages like this!

Here's how

Crop the photos as you like, using a corner rounder, decorative-edge scissors, and templates if you like. Mount some photos on scrapbook papers and trim $1/8$- to $1/2$-inch borders or cut mounting paper into a flower shape.

1. Use a glue stick to glue paper triangles in the corners of each background page. Arrange and glue photos in place.

2. Use a dragonfly stencil to make a shape in a color that shows up on the background. Cut out and add details with a marking pen. Use crafts glue to glue on seed beads for eyes and to decorate the wings. Glue the decorations on the background.

3. Decorate the page with wire words, stickers, and jewels. Trim the floral sticker centers with jewels or beads. Let the glue dry.

HANGIN' OUT

What you need

- 3 photos; ruler
- 12-inch squares of card stock in pink and mauve
- Card stock in white, purple, and teal
- 4¾ × 11½-inch strip of coordinating plaid paper
- 1-inch alphabet punch and swirl punch
- Scissors
- Paper trimmer
- Computer and printer
- Glue stick

Here's how

To create the background, glue the plaid paper across the bottom of the pink card stock, leaving ⅛ inch on the bottom and sides. Trim the photos as you wish. Mount the photos on white card stock and trim narrow borders. Mount one of

June 8, 2003
I was so excited to finally be with Mallory after not seeing her since 3rd grade, almost three years ago! We were laughing and playing car...
while we stayed up late on our second night of vacation. I tau...
how to do logic puzzles and she taught me how to play Liar, I...
game. My cousin and I both love big, puffy Cheetos so we at...
our fingers turned orange!

the photos again on mauve card stock and trim wide borders.

1. Cut a 5/8-inch strip from mauve card stock and glue it 3¾ inches from the top edge of the background card stock.

2. Glue one photo on the mauve strip, ¼ inch from the right edge of the background. Overlap and glue the other photos to the background.

3. Using a computer, print journaling on white card stock and trim into a rectangle. Mount on teal card stock and trim narrow borders. Glue in the lower left corner of the plaid paper.

4. Punch out the headline from purple card stock and the swirls from teal. Glue the letters and swirls to the background.

Here's a tip for you!

When you trim papers, keep the scraps! Paper strips, squares, rectangles, triangles, and other shapes come in handy for making quick pages. You can use the papers for borders, mounting photos or journaling, and more. To keep the paper scraps organized, group them by color and store them in envelopes. This will keep them flat and will save you valuable scrapping time!

A slice OF summer 2

Second Grade Class Picnic
May, 2000

We all had a great time at the picnic at John's house! We were ready for summer vacation to start, and it was fun to play in the tent. These are pictures of my class, Rachel, Madison, and me, and Jill with K.T. I'll miss my friends and teacher over the summer! 1

3

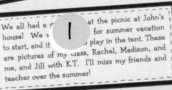

4

A picnic with friends is guaranteed to be a happy topic for a scrapbook creation!

What you'll need

Photos; 12-inch square of white card stock; ruler

Card stock in red, lime green, white, and black

Watermelon theme borders; die-cut title

Small heart punch

Scissors or paper trimmer

Black fine-line marking pen

White marking pen

Computer and printer

Glue stick

Here's how

For the background, glue watermelon borders at the bottom of the white card stock square, leaving 1/8 inch of white at the bottom edge and between the borders. Crop photos into rectangles. Glue the photos on white card stock and trim narrow borders. Mount photos on color card stock and trim.

1 Use a computer to print journaling and a main photo caption on white paper. Trim the copy blocks, mount on black card stock and trim narrow borders. Glue the journaling on the background. Glue the caption on one photo.

2 Glue the title to red card stock and trim into a rectangle. Glue this piece on green card stock and trim a narrow border. Cut two 1 1/2-inch squares from red card stock and two from green. Turn to make diamond shapes. Overlap the green diamonds on the red. Arrange the shapes on either side of the headline and glue in place.

3 To make seeds, punch hearts from black paper and cut in half. Use a white marking pen to add highlights. Glue to page.

4 Use a black marking pen to make dotted line borders on the red mats and white journal blocks.

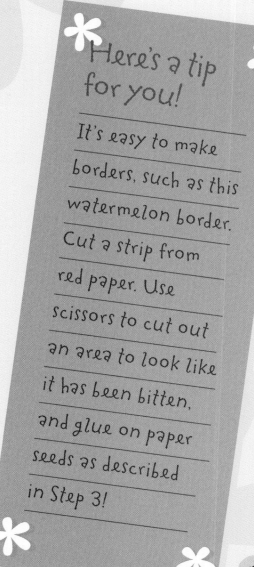

Here's a tip for you!

It's easy to make borders, such as this watermelon border. Cut a strip from red paper. Use scissors to cut out an area to look like it has been bitten, and glue on paper seeds as described in Step 3!

friends

What you need

Photos; ruler

Two 12-inch squares of purple print background paper

Pink and white stripe paper

Pink die cut letters

Vellum stickers in girl and flower motifs

Black number stickers

Paper cutter or scissors

Circle cutter

Computer and printer

Glue stick

Here's how

Crop the photos as you wish, using a circle cutter for some of the photos. Mount the photos on striped paper and trim narrow borders.

The road to a friends house is never long

Nothing can come between true friends

Make a couple of bright pages devoted to good ol' goofing around!

KIDS

02-03

4

2

A friend is one who knows all about you and likes you anyway

1 Place the background sheets side by side. Arrange the die cut letters at the top and glue in place.

2 Use a computer to print out messages about friendship (the ones we used are listed below). Print out the messages on white paper, using pink ink. Trim narrow borders around the messages.

3 Arrange the photos and printed messages on the pages. Glue them in place.

4 Press on stickers where there are open spaces. Record the date below the title using black number stickers.

The road to a friend's house is never long.

Nothing can come between true friends.

A friend is one who knows all about you and likes you anyway.

ABC Friends

What you'll need

for the cover

10¼×8¾-inch black scrapbook paper and a scrapbook with a black cover; ruler

Cream color card stock

Black mulberry (with fibers) paper

Stamp-style A, B, and C letters

"Friends" black die cut

Black chalk

1-inch-wide ivory grosgrain ribbon

Pencil; scissors

Corner rounder; glue stick

Here's how

1. Cut a 6½×2½-inch piece from cream card stock. Round the corners and rub chalk on the edges. Glue the die cut to the center.

2. Glue the letters to mulberry paper. Carefully tear away the mulberry paper at the letter edges, letting some of the black paper show. Cut three 1½×1¾-inch cream rectangles. Glue each mulberry paper to a cream rectangle. Glue the pieces on the cover as shown.

Because friends mean the world, create an A, B, C book to organize their photos.

What you'll need

for the pages

Photos; ruler; card stock in cream and white

Black and cream striped scrapbook papers

Black mulberry (with fibers) paper

Vellum; black chalk

Stamp-style letters

Corner rounder, if desired; pencil

Templates in round and oval shapes

Computer and printer

Scissors; glue stick

Here's how

Crop the photos. Use a corner rounder if you wish. To make a circle or oval, trace around a template and cut out shape. If you wish, glue photos to one of the papers or card stock and trim narrow borders. Mount a second time and trim a border. When using mulberry paper, tear the edges to get an uneven look.

1 Make up or find quotes or sayings about friendship. Type them on a computer using a variety of letter styles. Print on white paper. Chalk the edges. Cut out sayings, chalk the edges, and glue to cream, black, or striped papers; trim borders.

2 On each right-hand page, place a letter sticker. Vary the letter placement on the page, and mount it on papers if you wish.

3 Glue a friend's photo on the letter page that begins his or her name, such as Ashley on the A page. For each friend, print a journal box devoted to them. Include things like how you met and why you're glad she is your friend. If you have pages without photos, use those to say something about friendship. Arrange and glue the papers to the background.

Girl Power

Chatting, playing, eating, acting silly—sleepovers rule!

Ashley

Friends Forever

Girl Power

Taylor

JANA

Wild & Crazy

CHICKS RULE !

You GO girl !

24

What you'll need

Photos; ruler

12-inch square of white card stock

Card stock in purple, lavender, turquoise, yellow, light green, bright green, lime green, and light pink

White paper

Sticker phrases with clear backgrounds

Black marking pen

Paper cutter or scissors

Computer and printer

Glue stick

Here's how

Crop the photos to show the most important parts of each photo. Look at the page, left, to see the three horizontal rows of photos and how pieces are trimmed to line up evenly. Mount the photos on colored card stock and trim narrow borders. For one of the center photos, cut the card stock larger to leave room for names.

1 Use a computer and print out friends' names and phrases in color on white paper. Trim around words. Mount words on color card stock and trim narrow borders. If you like, cut out two background pieces from card stock and glue to word, as shown in the upper left corner behind the name Ashley.

2 Press stickers on color card stock and trim. Use a marking pen to add dotted line frames around some of the colored card stock.

3 Arrange the photos and the lettering. Glue to white card stock. Stick more word stickers over the photos, placing them around the faces in the photo.

Here's a tip for you!

Did you know you can make your own stickers using a computer? Look in an office supply store for printable labels. They come in colors and clear, so you can create stickers that say anything you wish!

25

Bathing Beauties

What you'll need

Photos; two 12-inch squares of water print paper; ruler

Card stock in yellow and purple

Headline die cut

Vellum stickers in floral and beach themes

Fine-line marking pens in black and purple

Templates in oval and round shapes; pencil

Paper cutter or scissors

Corner rounder; glue stick

Here's how

Crop the photos to show your fun-in-the-sun activities. To make round or oval cuts, trace the template and cut out the shape. Round the corners of straight-cut photos. Mount some of the photos on colored card stock and trim narrow borders.

2 Bathing Beauties   July 2001

Keely tiring to ski

Keely skiing

Saylorville Lake!

Whether you and your friends hit the lake, the ocean, or the pool, these scrapbook pages are swimming with ideas!

Laura

Me

Taylor & I

Keely

1. Taylor, Laura, & Keely having a great time at the lake!

Life's a beach

Laura & I

1. For the corner accents, cut triangles from purple card stock and smaller triangles of yellow. Glue the yellow triangles in the center of the purple triangles. Glue a photo over the smaller triangle, allowing a narrow border of yellow to show.

2. Glue the headline die cut to yellow card stock and trim a narrow border. Glue the headline, corner accents, and photos in place.

3. To fill in open areas, press stickers between and overlapping photos slightly.

4. Write journaling as you wish, using the photo edges as guides.

Having a Ball

What you'll need

Photos; ruler

Two 12-inch squares of ball print paper

Card stock in yellow, royal blue, and red

"Having A Ball" die cut

Acetate

Glitter; paper punch

3½-inch circle template

Scissors; foam tape

Computer and printer

Glue stick

Here's how

Crop the photos in rectangles. Mount the photos on yellow card stock and trim narrow borders. Mount the photo on royal blue card stock and trim narrow borders.

When you get silly with your girlfriends, catch it on film!

For Christina's Birthday Jackie, Shana, and I blindfolded her and took her on a car ride to Chuck E. Cheese. We had the whole place to ourselves. So naturally we ended up in our favorite place, the ball pit

1. Use a computer to print journaling and date on yellow card stock and trim into rectangles. Mount the blocks on royal and trim narrow borders.

2. Glue the title on yellow card stock and trim close to the letters, leaving a narrow border. Mount again on royal and trim just beyond yellow.

3. To make the confetti-filled circles, trace around the circle template on each color of card stock twice. On one set, cut out the inside of the circle, leaving a $1/4$-inch ring.

4. To make the circles look overlapped, cut away part of the blue and red circles and tape (making crescent moons). Glue the card stock ring to acetate and trim around circle. Stick the foam ring to the card stock shapes. Punch dots from card stock. Place punched circles and glitter in circles. Press acetate circles on foam tape rings. Glue all pieces to the background.

Girls Just Wanna Have Fun

What you'll need

Photos; ruler

Two 12-inch squares of white card stock

12-inch square of green stripe paper

Card stock in white, dark pink, turquoise, and green

White paper

Flower and title die cuts

Green wide-tip marking pen

Foam adhesive spacers, such as Pop Dots

Paper cutter or scissors

Computer and printer

Glue stick

Here's how

Crop the photos. Mount the photos on white card stock and trim narrow borders. Mount some again on pink card stock and trim slightly wider borders.

Madison, Bailey, and Kallen
Adventureland – August 2001

Pretty flowers and bright colors are just the ticket
for scrapbooking this summertime outing!

The weekend after 4th grade started, I got to take 2 friends to Adventureland because I won an extra ticket as a prize for one of my Iowa State Fair entries. I chose to take my friends Madison Thompson and Kallen Kramer, who happen to be first cousins. We went in the evening and stayed really late. We rode lots of rides and also played some games. I won a little stuffed piggy wearing a blue ribbon that I immediately named "Hoink" after the Iowa State Fair mascot. Madison and Kallen both won Beanie Baby frogs. I love my Hoink and he reminds me of the fair!

Forever Friends

1 With the stripes running up and down, cut the striped paper in half. Glue one striped paper to the inside edge of each background piece of card stock.

2 Cut two ½-inch strips from turquoise card stock. Glue the strips 1 inch from the top edge of background pieces.

3 Cut turquoise triangles for the outer corners and glue in place, leaving about ⅛-inch of background edge showing.

4 Using a computer, print journaling on white paper. Use a marking pen to make dashed lines around the edges. Cut into rectangles. Mount on pink paper. Trim narrow borders.

5 Cut out a few leaves from green card stock. Draw details with a green marking pen.

6 Arrange and glue all pieces in place, using foam spacers to raise some of the flowers.

Mall Scavenger Hunt

What you'll need

Photos; ruler

Two 12-inch squares of pink card stock

12-inch square of bright pink polka-dot paper

Card stock in white, bright pink, black

¾-inch black alphabet stickers

Die cuts in words, girls, and heart motifs

Paper cutter or scissors

Computer and printer

Glue stick

Here's how

Crop the photos. If you wish, cut a photo up and down and glue a piece to each page so the photo lines up across the pages. Mount some of the photos on white card stock and trim narrow borders. Mount some photos again on pink and black wider borders.

When a group of girls hits the mall, it's a blast no matter what the occasion!

November, 2002

outrageous

girl

Jill's 11th birthday, she had a scavenger hunt at Merle Mall. The eight of us divided into two groups and set off ourselves with $20, a list, and a camera. We had to find buy, I might add) each of the items on our list and meet at Dairy Queen in one hour. We had to find a shopping a napkin, something fuzzy, something green, something ly, something that smells good, something you put on hands, biggest item, and smallest item. We could take y pictures as we went along. We each got to keep one or of our purchases. We had a great time!

1 Cut two 5x11¾-inch pieces from polka-dot paper. Glue one strip to the bottom of one pink card stock background. Glue the other strip to the right side of the remaining pink card stock. Cut out black triangles and glue one in each outer corner.

2 Use a computer to print journaling on white card stock. Trim around the words. On the right side, trim a wavy line. Mount the journal block on bright pink card stock. Trim a narrow border. Print the date of the event on white and trim around the lettering. Mount on bright pink and black; trim narrow borders.

3 Press the M sticker on polka-dot paper and trim into a square. Mount again on white and trim. Glue the M block to the upper corner of the left page. Press the remaining title letters in place across the top. Arrange and glue the photos, die cuts, and journaling in place.

Piano Pals

Girls that PLAY together, STAY together!

Piano Pals

3

Special Friendship

2

Kindness

Us

June, 2002
This spring, I missed my piano recital because I had strep throat for the first time. My piano partner, Brynn Schmidt, is moving to New York, and this would have been our last recital to play together (Brynn had to play the duet with our teacher, Mrs. Caninel). So we invited Brynn over and videotaped us playing together. As always, we had fun playing the piano and goofing around! It was really hard to say good-bye to her, and it will be REALLY sad having to go to piano lessons each week without her!

1

What you'll need

Photos; ruler

12-inch square of white card stock

Card stock in bright pink, bright yellow, lavender, bright green, and white

White paper

¾-inch black alphabet stickers

Friendship-theme tags

Scissors

Paper trimmer

Computer and printer

Glue stick

Here's how

To create the background, cut 5⅝-inch squares from the pink, yellow, lavender, and green card stocks. Glue the squares on the white card stock background, leaving equal white space between each of the squares. Crop photos as you wish. Four photos work well for this grid-type of design. Mount the photos on white card stock and trim narrow borders. Mount two photos on color card stock and trim. Arrange the photos so the two matted with a color border are opposite each other. Overlap the photos a little bit and glue onto the background.

1 Use a computer to print journaling on white paper. Trim the copy block.. Mount the journaling on yellow card stock, and trim a narrow border. Glue the journal block on the background.

2 Cut out and put together the layers of the tags, if needed. Glue the tags to the background.

3 Use alphabet stickers to spell the title across the top of the page. Trim a motif from an extra tag and place by the title.

Here's a tip for you!

You can create tags to match any theme. To make a tag, cut a paper rectangle, clip two corners, and punch a hole in that end. Thread string through the hole, and glue small items on the tag or write a label.

Party, Party, Party!

What you'll need

- **Photos; ruler**
- **Two 12-inch squares of print background papers**
- **Two 12-inch squares of check background papers in cool colors**
- **3 more print scrapbook papers in patterns you like**
- **Solid papers in a color and white**
- **Beaded letters to spell "Party"**
- **Stickers or die cuts of balloons, stars, and word bubbles**
- **Alphabet stickers**
- **Tiny buttons**
- **Flower paper punch**
- **Paper trimmer; scissors**
- **Decorative-edge scissors, if you wish**
- **Corner rounder**
- **Oval and hexagon templates, if you wish**
- **Glue stick**

When it's your big day, take lots of photos to recall the fun celebration.

Here's how

Crop the photos, using a corner rounder, decorative-edge scissors, and templates as you wish. Mount photos on print papers and trim narrow borders.

1 Cut two 9-inch squares from check paper. Angle each paper on a background and glue in place. Arrange and glue photos on background.

2 To make the packages, cut small rectangles and squares from print papers. Cut colorful strips for ribbons. Punch flowers for bows and background. Glue pieces together, adding a button to each flower center. Glue packages and extra flowers to background.

3 Glue wire "Party" to white paper. Cut out around letters. Glue to color paper; trim a narrow border. Glue title to the top of the left page. Glue balloon and stars around title.

4 Use alphabet stickers and word bubbles to add words.

Hippie Birthday

HIPPIE BIRTHDAY

groovy

For my 9th birthday, I had a late-60's party and asked everyone to come dressed like a hippie. We tie-dyed t-shirts, listened to 60's music, and had 60's food (like Tang and fondue). We decorated my room with my mom's old love beads and posters! These are pictures of my friends, face painting signs, and getting ready to have rainbow cake. My mom and dad even dressed up! We had an awesome time!

Make a groovy page that uses a play on words for the title.

What you'll need

Photos; ruler

12-inch squares of lavender, bright pink, white, and purple card stock

11½ ×5-inch piece of floral purple paper

White paper

¾-inch black alphabet stickers

Girls in a car, "groovy," and floral die cuts

Foam adhesive spacers, such as Pop Dots

Scissors; paper trimmer

Computer and printer

Glue stick

Here's how

To create the background, center and glue the floral purple paper ⅛-inch from the bottom of the lavender background card stock. Glue a ½×12-inch pink strip ⅛ inch from the left edge of the background paper. Crop the photos as you wish. Mount the photos on white card stock and trim narrow borders. Mount to purple or pink card stock and trim.

1. Glue the car die cut in the lower right corner.

2. Using a computer, print journaling on white paper. Cut around copy block using a wavy cut. Mount the journaling on pink card stock and trim a narrow border. Glue the journaling to the left of the car.

3. Arrange photos on the background. Glue to page.

4. Glue the "groovy" die cut to pink paper and trim a narrow border. Glue the die cut on the background above the car.

5. Use alphabet stickers to spell the title across the top of the page. Decorate with floral die cuts, using spacers on some of the flowers to raise them from the page.

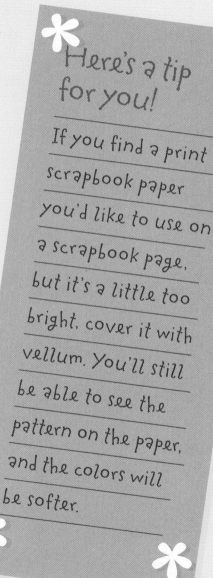

Here's a tip for you!

If you find a print scrapbook paper you'd like to use on a scrapbook page, but it's a little too bright, cover it with vellum. You'll still be able to see the pattern on the paper, and the colors will be softer.

Monopoly Marathon

MONOPOLY

MARATHON

1

COMMUNITY CHEST

CHANCE

2

TITLE DEED
PARK PLACE

RENT $35.
With 1 House $175.
With 2 Houses 500.
With 3 Houses 1100.
With 4 Houses 1300.
With HOTEL $1500.
Mortgage Value $175.
Houses cost $200. each
Hotels, $200. plus 4 houses

If a player owns ALL the Lots of any Color-Group, the
rent is Doubled on Unimproved Lots in that group.
©1935 Hasbro, Inc.

20 MONOPOLY
20
DELUXE EDITION
20

3

40

Here's a super-simple page design that works for any kind of board game.

What you'll need

Photos; ruler

12-inch square of white card stock

Card stock in royal blue and yellow

Blue chalk

Flat paper game pieces

Computer and printer

Scissors

Glue stick

Here's how

Crop the photos as you wish. For the top photo, use a photo of the game and cut it into four vertical strips. Glue all the photos to colored card stock and trim narrow borders.

1. Print the title on white in two vertical strips. Trim into bands. Use chalk to shade the outer edges of the title blocks. Glue to photo border.

2. Arrange photos on the page. Glue in place.

3. Glue the game cards on the page.

Here's a tip for you!

Shop in discount stores and bargain sections of toy departments for decorations for your scrapbook pages. For little cost you can find such items as play money, stickers, trading and playing cards, gift tags, labels, greeting cards, wrapping paper, name tags, place cards, and other flat items that will add personality to your scrapbook designs!

More Friends Titles

Here are some really neat titles for your scrapbook pages! Color copy them so you can use them again and again (and share them with friends)!

Friends are the flowers in life's garden.

Friendship Rules!

Friends, friends, friends!

My Friends are the BEST!

Make new friends but keep the old, one is silver and the other's gold.

My friends KNOW me (and love me anyway)!

Friendships are the best thing on earth.

My friends mean the world to me.

I'm thankful for friends!

Hanging Out with My Buddies

Pals...Buddies...Friends...Partners in Crime!

Through it all...we're friends!

Thanks, Buddy!

My Group of Pals

Me and My Friends

43

It's All About

My School

45

Bailey's Art

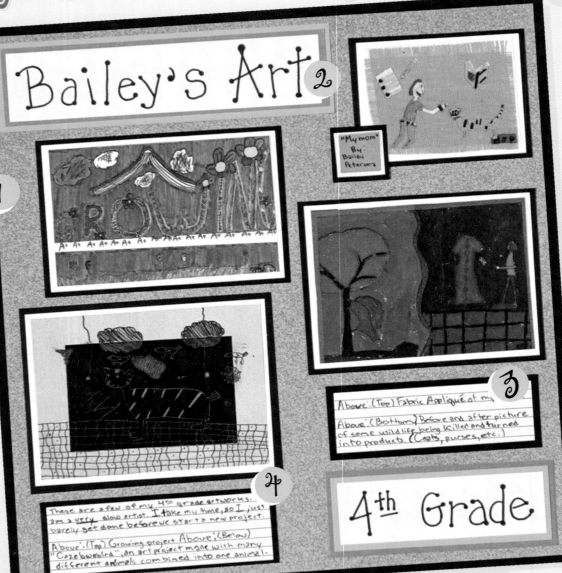

Bailey's Art ②

"My mom"
By:
Bailey
Peterson

①

③

Above: (Top) Fabric Appliqué of my,

Above: (Bottom) Before and after picture
of some wildlife being killed and turned
into products. (Coats, purses, etc.)

④

These are a few of my 4th grade artworks.
I am a very slow artist. I take my time, so I just
barely get done before we start a new project.

Above: (Top) Growing project Above: (Below)
"Camelwebird", an art project made with many
different animals combined into one animal.

4th Grade

As you soar through each grade, keep a record of your artwork to show your creative side.

What you'll need

Reduced color copies of your artwork; ruler

12-inch square of black card stock

11½-inch square of tan speckled scrapbook paper

Paper in white, black, blue, and turquoise

Ruled white paper

Black fine-line marking pen

Paper cutter or scissors

Glue stick

Here's how

Crop the color copies of your artwork up to the edge of your art. Mount the copies on white paper and trim narrow borders. Mount again on black paper and trim narrow borders.

1. Glue the speckled paper in the center of the black card stock square.

2. Use a marking pen to print the title and grade on white paper. Cut out the title and date. Mount the title on blue paper. Trim narrow borders. Mount on turquoise paper and trim again. Do the same with the date, mounting on turquoise first.

3. Use ruled paper to write journaling about each piece of artwork. Cut out and glue on black paper. Trim narrow borders.

4. Arrange and glue the title, artwork, journaling, and date to the background.

Here's a tip for you!

For extra special artwork, mount it behind a purchased mat. Mats are available where frames are sold in discount, crafts, and art stores. You can buy them in several styles, sizes, colors, and shapes.

A Night in Venice

"A Night in Venice"

The Associated Student Body

Of

Point Loma High School

requests the pleasure of your company at

"A Night in Venice"

on Saturday, the first of February

Two thousand and three

at eight o'clock in the evening

San Diego Marriott Hotel & Marina

Design a page that's almost as pretty as your prom dress!

what you need

Photo; ruler

Two 12-inch square of dark blue card stock

12-inch square of red mesh paper

Metallic gold crinkled paper

Prom invitation

Laser-cut gondola; glitter moon die cut

Metallic gold star and alphabet stickers

Scissors; glue stick

here's how

1. Crop the photo if needed. Mount the photo on gold crinkle paper; trim $1/2$-inch borders.

2. Glue red mesh paper over one square of blue card stock. Cut a wavy strip from remaining blue square and adhere to bottom of red mesh paper.

3. Glue the mounted photo and invitation to the background. Stick the title and glue the die cuts in place. Stick stars randomly around page.

Here's a tip for you!

Proms and other special dances and events often have theme-related decorations that are available at paper supply (party) stores. As soon as you know the theme, check the store for small decorations, such as napkins, invitations, buttons, die cuts, streamers, mobiles, place cards, and other flat items you can use on your scrapbook page.

Hats Off!

What you'll need

Photos; ruler; glue stick

Two 8½×11-inch pieces of textured paper in a school color

Iridescent white vellum

Card stock in a school color

Graduation announcement and name card

Graduation cap die cuts, 3 black and 3 white

Silver cord; ⅛-inch silver stripe stickers

1-inch metallic lettering in school color

Scissors; paper trimmer

Double-stick tape

Thick white crafts glue

Here's how

Crop photos; glue to colored card stock and/or vellum, as you wish. Trim narrow borders.

1 Press stripe stickers ⅛ inch from each outside edge of textured paper.

Celebrate graduation or another important event with special colors and textures.

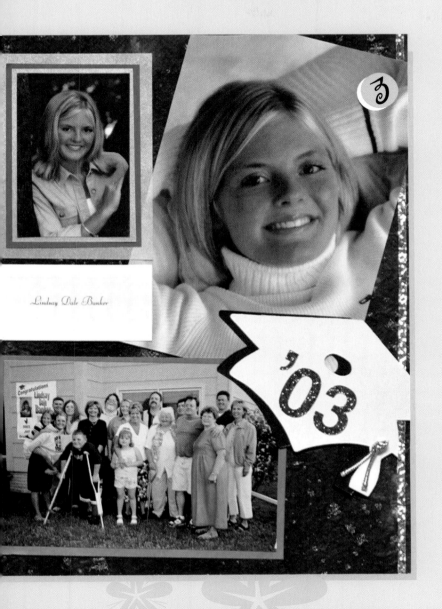

Lindsay Dale Banker

2 For the title, cut a 2³/₄×7-inch piece from colored card stock; glue to the top of the left page, leaving borders at the top and left. Cut a 2¹/₂×4¹/₄-inch piece from vellum. Use two strips of double-stick tape to mount it on the card stock rectangle. The tape will show through the vellum appearing as stripes. Glue a black cap to the left side of the title. Glue a white cap on top, shifting it slightly to create a shadow.

3 Glue the photos, invitations, and name card on the background; trim if needed.

4 Use alphabet stickers to spell "HATS OFF" in title box. On remaining white caps, use stickers to record school initials and the year. Glue white caps to black, offsetting slightly. Glue to page.

5 Glue cording around the title box. For tassels, knot two strands of cord together, trim, and glue to each cap.

Go Bananas

What you'll need

- **Photos; ruler**
- **Two 12-inch squares of print paper in a school color**
- **Card stock in a contrasting color**
- **Vellum**
- **Die cut letters, bananas, and cheerleader**
- **Small eyelets to match background paper**
- **Eyelet tool**
- **Dark brown chalk**
- **Fine-line brown marking pen**
- **Scissors**
- **Computer and printer**
- **Glue stick**

Here's how

Using the pages, right, as a guide, crop the photos in squares and rectangles. Mount all but one of the photos on card stock. Trim narrow

Form the **banana**, form, form the banana,
Form the banana, form, form the banana.

Peel the banana, peel, peel the **banana**,
Peel the banana, peel, peel the banana.

Go bananas, go, go bananas,
Go **bananas**, go, go bananas.

Form the **orange**, form, form the orange,
Form the orange, form, form the orange.

Peel the orange, peel, peel the **orange**,
Peel the orange, peel, peel the orange.

Squeeze the orange, squeeze, squeeze the orange,
Squeeze the **orange**, squeeze, squeeze the orange.

"Go Bananas" is a chant the cheerleaders
learned at camp. The kids at the games
would go "bananas" over it.

Rah, rah, sis-boom-bah! You did the cheers without a flaw!

the potato, form, form the potato,
m the potato, form, form the potato.

l the potato, peel, peel the **potato**,
el the potato, peel, peel the potato.

ash the potato, mash, mash the potato,
ash the potato, mash, mash the potato.

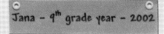

Jana – 9th grade year – 2002

Form the **corn**, form, form the corn,
Form the corn, form, form the corn.

Shuck the co   huck the **corn**,
Shuck the co   shuck the corn.

Pop the corn, pop, pop the corn,
Pop the **corn**, pop, pop the corn.

BANANAS

borders or trim much larger to leave room for journaling. For a variation, such as in the upper right corner, cut three ⅞-inch-wide strips to back a photo.

1. Use chalk and a marking pen to color the parts of the banana die cuts. Make dotted lines with the marking pen to separate the peel from the banana. Use chalk to create the look of shadows. Glue bananas in place on photo mats or plain card stock.

2. Using a computer, print journaling on vellum and trim into rectangles to fit various card stock backgrounds. To attach the journal blocks, use an eyelet in each corner following the instructions on the eyelet packaging.

3. Glue the title on the background papers. Glue the mounted photos and journaling, and cheerleader die cut on the background.

Track and Field

What you'll need

Photos; ruler

Two 12-inch squares of green and brown track paper

Card stock in yellow or a school color

Die cut of school name

"Track & Field" sticker

Small track-theme sticker

Paper cutter or scissors

Oval and circle template

Black fine-line marking pen; pencil; glue stick

Here's how

Crop the photos to show the important parts. Leave enough of the track setting in the photos to carry out the theme. To make round or oval cuts, trace around the template and cut out the shapes. Mount all but three of the photos on card stock and trim narrow borders.

This bold design will have you sprinting for your scrapbook papers!

1. Stick the "Track & Field" sticker on the right page, centered top to bottom and about 1/8 inch from the left edge.

2. Angle and glue the school die cut on the left page.

3. Stick a small sticker on card stock and trim to a small rectangle. Outline the rectangle and the school die cut with a short dashed line.

4. Glue the photos and the mounted sticker to the background paper.

5. Print journaling around photos wherever you like.

Soccer

Show spirit for your team with this cool layout that includes your teammates' signatures!

What you'll need

Photos; ruler

Two 12-inch squares of white card stock

One 12-inch square of card stock in one of your team colors

Card stock in a contrasting team color or a color you like, and white

Die cuts in grass, soccer balls (one large, two small), and jersey designs

Die cut letters, 3/4-inch for title and name on jersey and 2-inch for jersey number

Paper cutter or scissors

Black fine-line marking pen; glue stick

Here's how

Crop the photos into rectangles. Mount two of the photos on different colors of card stock and trim narrow borders.

SOCCER 1

JOHNSON 40

5

Aerielle Smith #86!
Chelsy Lee #4
Whitney Ferin =
Brittnie Letting #56!
Michelle Varnum #30!
Katie Kasper #83!
Erica Willey #14
Kelly Kasper #77!
Emily Falk #8
Annie Heyermann #7 !!
Brielle Neumann #9
Kristi Fisher #43 !!
Allie Haight #57
Kerry Meighan #40
Angie Pick #11

4

☉2002☉

1 Cut two 1½-inch wide strips from colored card stock. Glue a strip at the top of each white card stock page, about ¼ inch from the top edge.

2 Glue the die cut grass at the bottom of each page.

3 Arrange the photos on one page, overlapping as you like. Glue in place.

4 Cut a 3½×6-inch piece of white paper. Ask your teammates to sign their names and jersey numbers on the paper. Mount the white paper on colored card stock and trim a border. Glue the signatures at an angle on the left page, as shown.

5 Glue the jersey on the left page. Glue the die cut balls and letters onto the background.

Student Driver

What you'll need

Photos; ruler

Two 8½ ×11-inch pieces of blue background card stock

Two 8½ ×11-inch pieces of grass-pattern paper

Solid gray, yellow, brown, black, and white papers

Marking pens in black and white

Scissors

Glue stick

To create photos to personalize scrapbook pages, take your camera to unexpected places and events, such as driver's ed class.

Take photos to tell a story. Rather than searching for perfect art elements, photograph your own decorations, such as road signs and a "student driver" sign to use for the title.

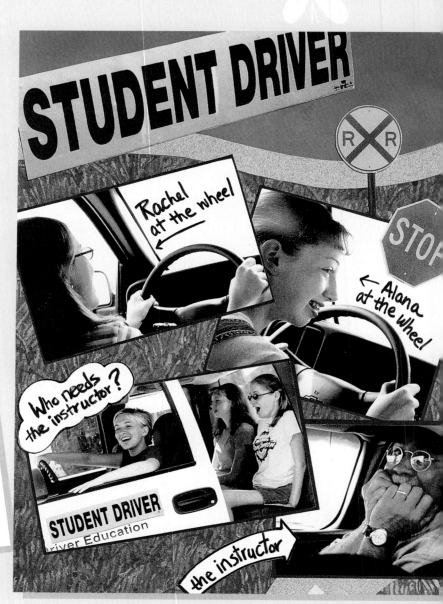

Here's a topic every teen will want to remember, and many parents may want to forget!

Here's how

1. Crop and cut around photos as you wish. Mount the photos on black paper; trim narrow borders. Carefully cut out road signs, cutting away the posts.

2. Cut grass papers for the lower portions of the pages using a wavy cut. Cut curved strips of gray paper, and a dotted yellow line for the road.

3. Cut varying lengths of signposts from brown paper.

4. Cut cloud shapes and arrows from white and yellow papers for journaling. Use a black marking pen to write journaling in the cutouts. Glue the paper pieces on the background pages.

Swing Choir

1

Andy
and
Lizzy

3 Ali, Liz, Jessie, and Hallie
singing "Mr. Sandman"

Singing
"Zoot Suit
Riot"

2

60

What you need

Photos; ruler

12-inch squares of striped and check card stock

Clear gel glue; blue fine-line marking pen

Glitter; scissors; glue stick

Here's how

Cut the stripe paper in half and glue it horizontally across the checked page. Crop the photos and choose one to cut around. Place these figures behind a rectangular photo. Glue the photos to the page.

1. For the title, write the words on the background paper using gel glue. While the glue is wet, sprinkle with glitter. Let the glue dry. Shake off extra glitter.

2. To make the music staff, use a marking pen to draw wavy lines. Add notes with glue and glitter. Let dry.

3. Use a marking pen to write journaling by photos.

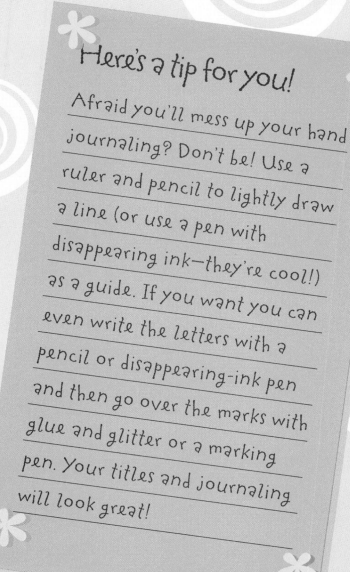

Here's a tip for you!

Afraid you'll mess up your hand journaling? Don't be! Use a ruler and pencil to lightly draw a line (or use a pen with disappearing ink—they're cool!) as a guide. If you want you can even write the letters with a pencil or disappearing-ink pen and then go over the marks with glue and glitter or a marking pen. Your titles and journaling will look great!

Regional Swim Meet

What you'll need

- **Photos**
- **Ruler**
- **Two 12-inch squares of water print paper**
- **Red card stock**
- **Alphabet stickers in 1¼-inch red and ½-inch silver**
- **Swim-theme border and die cuts**
- **Water-theme photo mat**
- **Adhesive foam spacers, such as Pop Dots**
- **Scissors**
- **Star punch**
- **Tape**
- **Glue stick**

Dive right in and make some pages that show off a talented swimmer ... you!

Crop the photos. Mount three of the photos on red card stock and trim narrow borders. Tape a photo behind the water-theme photo mat.

1 Press on the large red letters for the title, centering it on the two background pages. Use the silver letters to stick the date below the title.

2 Glue the border strips across the bottom of the pages.

3 Glue the rest of the pieces to the background, using adhesive spacers to attach the stars.

More School Titles

Label your school-theme pages with these awesome headlines!

* school Days *

I ♥ love school!

My teacher is waaay cool!

Teacher's pet? NOT!

Math is awesome, art is cool—I love everything that has to do with school!

Sr. High Rocks!

School parties put a smile on my face!

But after the bell rang. . .

Me & My Classmates!

My days at school

field trips are the best!

It's All About

My Family

My Family

What you'll need

Photos; ruler

Two 8½×11-inch pieces of white card stock

8½×11-inch pieces of card stock in blue, white, green, brown, and red

Vellum stickers in family member, lettering, and shrub motifs

Punches in leaf, butterfly, and swirl motifs

Scissors; fine-line black marking pen; glue stick

Here's how

Crop the photos and mount on white. Trim narrow borders. Mount the photos on blue and trim narrow borders.

1 Cut a lawn from green card stock. Glue lawn on the bottom of each white background page.

2 To make the tree, fold brown card stock in half.

Me in the backyard doing fall clean-up

Grandpa

Mom

Me

Create pages to celebrate some of the most important people in your life—your family!

Grandma

Dad

I love my family! We like to do things together. **3**

FAMILY

My cat

Dad and Mom in Pella **7**

Draw a tree and cut out. Cut the tree in two along the fold. Glue the tree in place, lining up the tree center with the inside edges of background. Glue the photos in place.

3 Draw a cloud on white card stock and cut out. Write journaling on the cloud; glue to the page.

4 Punch out 10 green leaves, three red butterflies, and one yellow swirl for the sun. Glue the leaves at the ends of the branches. Glue the butterflies on the white background. Glue the swirl in the upper left corner. Cut out yellow triangles to add sun rays. Glue around yellow swirl.

5 Place the shrub stickers.

6 Stick the remaining stickers on white card stock and trim. Glue the lettering to blue card stock; cut between the words. Draw a black border. Press stickers on page.

7 Use the marking pen to add journaling. Make dots and details using the marking pen.

Wild Thing

What you'll need

Photos; ruler; two 5½×7¼-inch pieces of brown card stock

Tan card stock; animal print and white paper

Paw print, mouse, and caption bubble stickers

¾-inch black alphabet stickers

Brown nubby string (fiber)

Scissors or paper trimmer

Decorative-edge scissors

Black fine-line marking pen

Glue stick

Here's how

Crop the photos as you wish. Glue the photos to white paper and trim borders.

1 Cut two ½×7¼-inch strips from tan card stock. Glue a strip across each brown background, ½ inch from the top. Press paw print stickers across strips.

No member of the family is more important than your cat or dog!

Tinsel
Christmas
Peterama

4

5

Aren't
I
FIERCE?

Thing

2 Cut a 4-inch square from animal print paper. Cut it in half, corner to corner, to make two triangles. Glue a triangle to each page, long edge of the triangle along the inside edge of the background paper.

3 Use decorative-edge scissors to cut small squares or rectangles (about 1-inch) from tan card stock. Stick an alphabet sticker in each square to spell the title. Use a marking pen to roughly outline each piece.

4 Cut two 1x1½-inch tags from tan card stock. Snip off the corners on one short end of each tag; poke a hole in these ends about ⅛ inch from the edge. Outline tags with black. Place a mouse sticker in the center of one tag. On the remaining tag, write the pet's name; press a pawprint sticker below it.

5 Glue items to the background. Write in a caption bubble and stick it on a photo.

Playin' Around

PLAYIN AROUND

Silly String

72

Even moms can get silly!

What you'll need

Photos

12-inch square of grass print paper

Card stock in yellow, turquoise, purple, bright pink, and white

Embroidery floss in yellow and turquoise

Fine-line marking pens

Aluminum foil

Chalks in yellow, pink, orange, blue, purple, and green

Paper trimmer

¾-inch letter punch

Glue stick

Here's how

Crop the photos into rectangles or squares. Mount the photos on different colors of card stock and trim narrow borders.

1 Punch out the letters for the headline from white card stock. Chalk each letter to add soft color.

2 For spray-string can, cut a 1x2⅛-inch rectangle from purple card stock. Cut a 1x½-inch piece from yellow card stock, cutting one long edge wavy. Glue onto the purple shape. Use marking pens to decorate the can. Cut a spray can shape top from aluminum foil.

3 Arrange the photos, lettering, and handmade die cut on the background. Before gluing in place, wrap with pieces of embroidery floss. Glue pieces to the background, catching the floss to secure it to the background.

Here's a tip for you!

Embroidery floss comes in hundreds of colors and is inexpensive. You can buy it at crafts, stitchery, and discount stores. Start collecting floss, then use it to trim your pages with color!

Tinsel

Tinsel, my first kitty, is so sweet. (Most of the time.) She likes to pose strangely. I think she's showing off for the camera.

February, 2003
Tinsel - Age 2

Tinsel

When you're adding family pages to your scrapbook, don't forget the kitty!

What you'll need

Photos; ruler

12-inch square of tan card stock

4×11½-inch black card stock

8½×9½-inch cat theme paper

Card stock in white and maroon

1½-inch black die cut letters

Black pawprint stickers

Paper cutter; scissors

Black fine-line marking pen

Glue stick

Here's how

Crop the photos to show different poses of your cat. Mount the photos on white card stock and trim narrow borders. Mount one photo again on maroon card stock and trim wider borders, allowing room for the paw print stickers on the left side of the mat.

1. Glue the black card stock to the tan card stock even with the bottom and ½ inch from the left edge. Glue the cat theme paper even with the top of the background sheet, ¾ inch from the right edge.

2. Use a ruler and marking pen to draw lines on white card stock. Use the lines as guides to print information about your pet. Place two paw print stickers on the card stock and trim just beyond the writing. Mount the journaling on maroon card stock; trim narrow borders.

3. Use the die cut lettering to spell your cat's name across the bottom of the tan card stock.

4. Cut two small hearts from maroon card stock; glue to the left of the lettering. Glue the photos and journaling on the page.

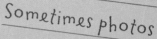

Here's a tip for you!

Sometimes photos of people or animals print with red eyes. If your photos have red in the centers of eyes, you can fix them with a red-eye pencil available at scrapbooking and photo stores.

Playing Ball

PLAYING BALL

June 2002

1

2

While at a family reunion in Sharrard we had a blast playing baseball. We lost most of the balls in the field by where we were playing.

3

Chris Amanda

Alex

Chad Ashley

It doesn't matter who wins the game, as long as your family has a blast pitching and hitting!

What you'll need

Photos, including the individual players

Ruler

12-inch square of white card stock

Red card stock

White paper

Red alphabet die cuts

Stickers of small baseballs, a glove, and a bat

Black fine-line marking pen

Scissors

Computer and printer

Glue stick

Here's how

Crop the photos as you wish. To make a photo stand out, mount it on red card stock and trim narrow borders. Trim the individual player photos close to the person photographed.

1. Glue on the red die cut letters for the title, placing the word "ball" below "playing."

2. Use a computer to print journaling on white paper. Trim just beyond the journaling. Mount journaling on red card stock. Trim narrow borders.

3. Glue the photos and journal box on the background, overlapping some of the photos slightly. Press baseball stickers at the ends of each headline letter. Press remaining stickers in place. Write the teammates names under each of their photos and record the date on the glove sticker.

Here's a tip for you!

Decorate large letters by placing small stickers, such as the baseballs, on the ends of the letters or by placing the stickers inside the letters. Try stickers of bugs, dots, hearts, or stars.

77

Backyard Campin'

BACKYARD CAMPIN'

June, 2001
One night, Dad and I decided to sleep in the tent out in the backyard. It started out as a warm night, but ... ning, we were cold-even with sweatshirts and b! ... en the birds woke us up REALLY early, so we gav ... went inside. I was so cold, I had a cup of coffee ... warm up!

Add punched-out characters to an organized page to give it personality.

What you'll need

Photos; ruler; 12-inch square blue card stock

Card stock in light blue, light green, white, brown, black, blue, rust, dark green, and peach

Black eyelets; eyelet tool

¾-inch black alphabet stickers

Punches for paper dolls

Scissors; paper trimmer

Black fine-line marking pen; glue stick

Here's how

Cut a 4x11¾-inch strip from light blue card stock. Glue the strip to the left side of the blue background, leaving ¼ inch on the left and bottom as a border. Crop photos as you wish. Mount one photo on white and green card stocks and trim narrow borders.

1 Cut a 2x8½-inch strip from light green. Glue strip to left side of background, ⅛ inch from the top and even with the left edge. Press alphabet stickers to the strip to spell title.

2 Cut a 2x6½-inch strip from light green. Glue the strip to the right side of the background, ½ inch from the bottom and even with the right edge.

3 Draw rules on white card stock. Print journaling using rules as guides. Trim block, allowing ½ inch on the left side. Cut a ½-inch-wide light green strip to apply to the left edge of the journal block. Trim even.

4 Glue photos in place, leaving room for journaling. Use eyelets to hold the journal box and title.

5 Punch out paper dolls and clothing. Glue on clothes. Use marking pen to draw faces and add clothing details. Glue one motif in the upper left and one in the lower right.

Here's a tip for you!

Eyelets come in all sorts of shapes, sizes, and colors! You can choose hearts, flowers, circles, squares, or other fun shapes. Check out the variety in scrapbooking and stamping stores.

Jill and Jana

What you'll need

- Photos; ruler
- Two 12-inch squares of lavender polka dot paper
- Vellum in lavender and purple
- Alphabet stickers
- Needle
- Thread or floss
- Purple and lavender buttons
- Two lavender tags
- Computer and printer
- Scissors; pencil
- Corner rounder
- Oval and circle templates
- Glue stick

Here's how

Crop the photos as you like. To make oval or circle shapes, trace the template on the photo and cut out. Use a corner rounder on straight-cut photos if you wish.

Christmas '91
Jill - 8 yrs.
Jana - 4 yrs.

Easter 1990

Easter 1991
Jill 7 ½ yrs.
Jana 3 ½ yrs.

Christmas 1992

1989

April '89
Jill - 5 ½ yrs.
Jana - 1 ½ yrs.

This picture was taken when Jill was in the hospital with appendicitis. It was Jeff's 10th birthday - 3/24/91. Jill was 7 ½ yrs. and Jana was 3 ½ yrs.

Sisters share a closeness no one else can understand.
A sister's always there
To give a hug or lend a hand.
Sisters are the best things in the whole wide world, it's true.
And that friendship is a blessing that lasts a lifetime through.

There's no one quite like a sister to brighten your world!

Sisters are special
From young ones to old,
God gave me a sister
more precious than gold.
We shared many secrets,
the same Mom and Dad,
we shared lots of clothes,
don't think I...
Our memories we cherish,
with love without end,
I'm glad you're my sister,
I'm glad you're my friend.

First day of school '94
Jill – 5th grade – 10 yrs.
Jana – 1st grade – 6 yrs.

2000
Jill 16 yrs.
Jana 12 yrs.

Ready for gymnastics

...picture was taken on the boat.
...was 6 yrs. old. As we were
...out of the cove we hit a big
...Jana went up and then came
...and hit the boat. Her front
were knocked loose. She had
...up for a few days.

Riding the wave runner at the Ozarks

Christmas 2001

Jana

1. Using a computer, print blocks of journaling on vellum. Carefully tear vellum around journaling.

2. Arrange the photos on the background. Glue in place, leaving room for the names.

3. Press a first initial sticker on each tag and tie a thread or floss through the hole. Glue onto background, leaving space for the rest of the letter stickers. Spell out the names using stickers.

4. To attach journaling, use simple stitches (straight or cross stitches) or tack by sewing on a button on one or more corners. (Ask an adult for help sewing, if needed!)

81

Me and Grandpa

What you'll need

Photos; ruler

Three 12-inch squares of blue and purple plaid scrapbook paper

Tag template

Alphabet and heart stickers

Blue eyelets; eyelet tool

Blue buttons; thread or floss; needle

Oval and circle templates

Corner rounder; scissors

Computer and printer

Glue stick

Here's how

Crop the photos as you wish. For the circle and oval shapes, trace around a template on photo and cut out. Glue all the photos to one sheet of the background paper and cut narrow borders.

1984

Diane Adams
964-1753

Let's play horsee, Grandpa!!
Jill-6 yrs.; Jana 2 yrs.; §
Amanda-18 mos.

Relaxing with Grandpa

Grandpa Johnson's Birthday
1985

1986

The delightful hues on these pages create an artistic background for a tagged title and treasured photos.

1 Write journaling on leftover paper scraps. Cut into irregular shapes. Draw a border of wiggly lines.

2 Trace the tag template on the background paper scraps, cutting a light and dark piece for each tag.

3 Plan the words and arrange the light and dark tag pieces. Cut out an irregular rectangle in the center of each tag top. Glue top tag piece to bottom. Press the alphabet stickers in the rectangle cut outs. Attach an eyelet through the top of each tag. Thread a fiber through each eyelet. Sew buttons across the top of each page, aligning above the tags. Tie the fibers around the buttons.

4 Glue the photos, journal boxes, and tags to the background. Press heart stickers to background.

More Family/Pets Titles

For those great pages devoted to your family, use these nifty blurbs for quick titles.

My Relatives are the Coolest!

We Are Family!

Family Time is Fun Time

Families that Play Together, Stay Together

Our Family Vacation

My brother. . . my friend.

My sister. . . my friend.

You're the Cat's Meow!

Purrrrrrr-fect Pet

HANDSOME HOUND

Pretty Pooch

FAMILY FUN

It's All About

My Travels

Summer vacations are all about family fun!

What you'll need

Photos, including a landscape for headline

Two 12-inch squares of light blue card stock

12-inch squares of card stock in white, dark blue, purple, and lavender

8½×11-inch pieces of colored paper in green, yellow, and orange

Black medium-tip marking pen; scissors

Computer and printer

Ruler; glue stick

Here's how

Crop the photos, cutting squares and rectangles. Mount some of the photos on white card stock and trim narrow borders. Group some pictures as a unit. Glue to white card stock and trim, leaving a narrow white border on the sides and top.

our vacation in

ARIZONA

at the Grand Canyon in July 200

hang on!

it's hotter than Iowa!

1

2

smile!

1 Tear two strips from white card stock. Glue to the top of the light blue card stock.

2 Tear a half circle sun from orange paper and rays from yellow paper. Tear wide strips of dark blue, purple, and lavender card stock. Arrange and glue the pieces across the pages as shown at left.

3 Tear a cactus from green paper. Glue to left page and trim at edge. To make flowers, cut shapes from orange and yellow. Glue a yellow center on each flower. Use scissors to clip the outer edges to make petals. Glue the flowers on the cactus. Use a marking pen to write journaling, and draw flower centers, cactus needles, sun details, and ground details.

4 For title, print bold computer letters; cut out. Trace around letters on a landscape photo, cut out, and glue on page. Write "our vacation in" above title and outline each letter on the right and bottom edge.

Flying High

Traveling can lead to new experiences, like trying out a new trampoline!

FLYING HIGH

Jana · August '00

What you'll need

Photos; 12-inch square of cloud print paper

Card stock in yellow, green, red, blue, and orange

12×3½-inch strip of grass print paper

Vellum sticker of girl jumping

Large trampoline die cut

¾-inch alphabet stickers in yellow and red

Black crafting wire

Black fine-line marking pen; tape

Small artists' paintbrush

Adhesive foam spacers, such as Pop Dots

Scissors; glue stick

Here's how

Crop the photos and mount on one or two colors of card stock. Trim narrow borders.

1 Glue the strip of paper grass to the bottom of the cloud background paper.

2 Cut the trampoline die cut to fit the page bottom.

3 To make springs, cut eighteen 1½-inch-long pieces of wire. Wrap each wire around the paintbrush handle. Tape the ends of 17 springs around the inner edge of the trampoline die cut. Tape the other wire ends to the trampoline. Use spacers to place the trampoline design at the bottom of the page.

4 Place the girl sticker in the top left corner of the page, gluing a spring under her. Glue photos to page.

5 Use a yellow sticker for the F of the title. Press the rest of the title letters on yellow; trim in irregular shapes. Overlap and glue, using a spacer for the first H in "high".

6 Write journaling using a fine-line marking pen.

Here's a tip for you!

Make your own cloud-like background by using white chalk on sky blue paper. You can also use chalk on solid papers to make stripes, dots, spirals, or any designs you like!

Camp

If you love roasting marshmallows and hanging out at a cabin, you'll love creating pages about camping.

What you'll need

Photos

12-inch squares of brown leaf-print paper

Solid color card stock

Brown card stock

Tan color paper

Paper trimmer

Black fine-tip marking pen

Brown marker

Scissors

Ruler

Glue stick

Church camp was great! The theme this year was FAITH FACTOR. Everyone had a good time and made a lot of new friends!

These are some of my best pictures. On the top is Mary, our councelor, on kitchen patrol. On the bottom are some of the girls, with our Pastor.

THE GIRLS OF CABIN #14

I made some new friends [in] my Cabin. We all had so [mu]ch fun together and didn't [wa]nt to leave. These are some [of] the girls.

Here's how

Crop the photos into shapes you like, using a paper trimmer or scissors. Glue photos to solid color card stock and trim narrow borders.

1 Arrange the photos to plan the placement and sizes of the journaling blocks. Cut pieces of tan color paper and mount onto brown card stock; trim narrow borders. Write journaling with markers.

2 To make woodlike letters and journal box mats, cut brown paper into several long, irregular pieces. Use a black marking pen to draw in wood texture lines. Glue all pieces to the background paper.

Golf

Use just the right papers and dimensional stickers for a page that's perfect FORE you!

What you'll need

Photos

12-inch square of argyle (diamond pattern) paper

Card stock in gold and gray

2-inch gray die cut letters

Dimensional golf stickers

Black fine-tip marking pen

Paper cutter or scissors

Corner rounder

Ruler

Glue stick

Here's how

Crop the photos to show the important parts of each. Round the corners using a corner rounder. Mount all photos on gray card stock and trim narrow borders.

1 For the title, cut a 2¼×11-inch strip from gold card stock. Using the die cut letters, glue "GOLF" across the gold strip. Center and glue the strip to the top of the argyle paper.

2 Glue the photos in place, angling some for interest.

3 Press golfing stickers to the background paper and title strip. Stick a golf ball in the center of O in "GOLF."

4 Use a black marking pen to write journaling around and on the photo mats. Draw dotted lines around letters, title box, and flags.

Here's a tip for you!

Whether you golf out on the big course or like to play putt-putt on the miniature greens, hang on to your scorecards. These little papers make great additions to a page devoted to golfing.

Cool Drinks

Cool Drinks

Cancún 1996

96

Half the fun of vacations is trying different foods and yummy drinks!

What you'll need

Photos; 12-inch square of yellow sand print paper

Card stock in yellow, red, yellow-orange, cream, green, and royal; vellum

Small pineapple and 1-inch alphabet die cuts

Chalk in black and brown

Permanent fine-line marking pen

Circle cutter; scissors

½ inch round punch; ruler

Paper crimper; glue stick

Adhesive foam spacers, such as Pop Dots

Here's how

Crop the photos. Mount one photo on royal paper and trim a narrow border. Cut a second shape from royal, slightly larger than the other photo.

1 To create a pineapple, cut a 6×8-inch rectangle from yellow paper. Round the edges to create a pineapple shape. Use brown chalk to add diagonal lines in both directions. Dot the diamond centers with black chalk.

2 To make the pineapple face, cut two 2½-inch circles from yellow-orange card stock using a circle cutter. Punch two ½-inch circles from red. Cut a 4×1¼-inch strip from cream for nose. Taper long edges. Cut a rectangle 2¾×1¼ inches. Round one long edge. Use spacers to attach face features.

3 To make straws, cut two ⅜×4-inch vellum strips. For each straw, use a paper crimper 1½ inches from one end.

4 For green leaves, cut nine long leaf shapes.

5 Glue on title letters. Glue the leaf ends and straw ends to the pineapple back; glue to background. Glue photos and die cut in place. Use marking pen to write journaling.

Here's a tip for you!

When you travel, keep a daily diary. Record restaurant names, foods and drinks you have, places you visit— everything you can about your trip. Refer to your notes to make journaling a breeze!

Road Trip

What you'll need

Photos

Two 12-inch squares of royal print paper

Red card stock

Die cut title, road, mini van, bus, and stop and one-way signs

Scissors

Computer and printer

Ruler

Glue stick

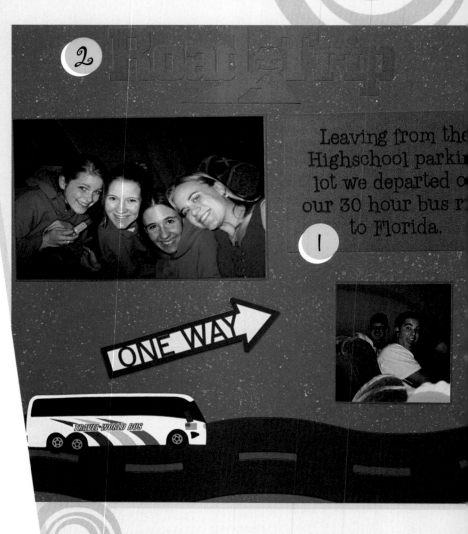

Leaving from the Highschool parking lot we departed on our 30 hour bus ride to Florida.

ONE WAY

A bus full of school buddies on the road to Florida ... what could be more fun?!

Here's how

Crop the photos in squares and rectangles. Mount the photos on red card stock and trim narrow borders.

1 Use a computer to print journaling on red card stock. Trim the journal box into a rectangle.

2 Glue the title at the top of the left page. Glue the photos in place, gluing four on the right page. (Notice how this page uses the same size squares and rectangles diagonally opposite each other for a balanced look.)

3 Glue the stop sign die cut in the center of the four photos on the right page. Glue the remaining die cuts to the background, using the pages, left, for ideas.

Making Waves

making WAVES

3

We went out tubing on the Lake of the Ozarks in 2001. Jana and Amanda went on the tube together and they had a blast making waves.

1

2

4

Lots of sun, deep blue water, and smiling faces are a winning combination for this outdoorsy page.

What you'll need

Photos

12-inch square of white card stock

Scrapbook papers in royal and turquoise

Blue vellum

Die cuts for title, kids boating, and child in a floating tube

White string

Oval and round templates

Scissors; pencil

Corner rounder

Computer and printer

Glue stick

Here's how

Crop the photos as you wish. For shapes with straight-edge cuts, round the corners. To cut ovals and circles, trace around the template you like and cut out.

1 To create journaling, print on blue vellum using a computer. Carefully tear around the journaling. Tear two more pieces for mounting small photos.

2 To make the waves, tear two narrow strips from royal paper. Glue to the bottom of the page.

3 Glue the title die cut to turquoise paper and trim a narrow border. Glue the turquoise paper to royal and trim another narrow border.

4 Arrange the photos, die cuts, and journal box on the page. Before gluing in place, place a string under the edges of the two boating die cuts to connect them.

Here's a tip for you!

Torn paper creates interesting shapes.

Trim your pages with such torn paper in the shape of:

- flowers
- leaves
- circles
- squares
- suns
- and stripes!

At the Ozarks

1

2

3

Always remember those special family vacations ... and smile for the camera!

What you'll need

Photos

12-inch square of yellow and pink polka-dot paper

Coordinating floral paper

Card stock in bright pink and white

Swimsuit and flower stickers

Alphabet punch

Scissors

Oval templates

Corner rounder

Glue stick

Here's how

Crop the photos. To make oval shapes, trace the template on the photos and cut out. Use a corner rounder on rectangle-cropped photos. Mount the photos on pink and white card stocks, trimming narrow borders.

1 Press the swimsuit stickers on pink card stock; trim into a small rectangle. Mount the stickered card stock on floral paper and trim a narrow border. Repeat with another piece of pink card stock.

2 Punch out the letters for the title from the floral paper. Mount on pink and trim narrow borders around each letter.

3 Cut a picture of your face to peek through one of the letters, such as the O in "Ozarks." Arrange the photos, title, and stickers; glue or press in place.

Here's a tip for you!

Scrapbook pages are much more interesting when there is variety in the photos. Notice how the page at left has one shot that's close up and others are taken from a distance. It works!

More Travel Titles

After you've unpacked your suitcase, use these fun titles and make some pages all about your trip!

What an Adventure!

I LOVE this Place!

The Great Outdoors

Vacations ROCK!

Are We There Yet?

Summers are meant for vacations

Me? Fly?

I LOVE TO FLY!

What a trip!

This is a blast!

Can we come back, and WHEN?

Buckle up, We're Heading Out!

All Aboard!

It's All About

Just Clownin' Around

When you want to create a lively scrapbook page, this easy-to-make design will do the trick.

What you'll need

- **Photo, about 6 inches square**
- **12-inch squares of dark and light color card stock for background**
- **Scraps of light color card stock for title**
- **2 colors of card stock for framing photo**
- **Colorful alphabet stickers**
- **Circle paper punch**
- **Star paper punch**
- **Decorative-edge scissors**
- **Ruler**
- **Glue stick**

Here's how

Crop the photo edges using decorative-edge scissors. Trim a piece of card stock the same size as the photo and two narrow strips the same length as the photo. Use a glue stick to apply the photo to the card stock square, offsetting it slightly to leave a 1/2-inch border at the top and right side. Cut another piece of card stock larger than the photo using decorative-edge scissors.

1. Use decorative-edge scissors to cut a wavy edge on the dark card stock.

2. Use circle and star punches to create designs around the edge of the dark card stock. Use a glue stick on the back and glue to the light card stock.

3. Apply alphabet stickers to the card stock scraps, curving the words. Cut around the words and glue them around the photo.

Here's a tip for you!

Use punched paper (like the blue background paper, opposite) to create greeting cards, gift tags, and scrapbook borders! Punches come in lots of shapes and can be bought at scrapbooking shops.

French Horn Solo

French Horn Solo Contest

Grandma accompanied me on piano.
I got a 1!

Go ahead — blow your own horn — you deserve it!

What You'll Need

Photo

2 contrasting tones of translucent vellum

Gold crinkle paper

Metallic gold wide- and fine-tip marking pens

Cream color pencil

Enlarged sheet of music to trace over

Paper trimmer

Ruler

Glue stick

Here's how

Crop the photo to the size you want it. The photo pictured, left, is 6×5 inches. Trim one color of vellum ½-inch larger than the photo. Trim the other vellum 9½ inches square.

1 To enlarge a sheet of music for decorative purposes, take it to a copy shop and enlarge it on a copier so the staff is approximately 1¼ inches high. Place the photocopy under the large vellum square and trace over it using a cream color pencil.

2 Use a wide-tip gold marker to add stripes around the edges of the smaller piece of vellum. Let dry. Mount the photo in the center of the vellum using a glue stick. Mount the small vellum piece in the center of the large square of vellum. Mount on the gold crinkle paper.

3 Write the title and journaling using a gold fine-tip pen.

Here's a tip for you!

Make your own crinkle paper to add texture to your paper crafts. Scrunch a piece of paper into a ball and then flatten it out. To smooth it, leave it under a heavy book before you use it.

Tap

Dance recitals are the best, and getting a bouquet of flowers makes it extra special!

Tap

1

Johnston Dance Recital – May, 2001
Central Campus, Des Moines, Iowa

4

3

2

When I was 8, I tapped my way to a great dance recital. I was thrilled to receive a bouquet of roses from Grandma + Grandpa for my hard work and as a reward for my wonderful and memorable performance!

5

DANCE
USA

What you'll need

Photos

12-inch square of white card stock

12×1½-inch strip of black card stock

Card stock to coordinate with dance outfit in photo, plus black and white

White paper

Black photo mat

Dance girl and decorative border die cuts

Eyelets in silver and black

Eyelet tool

Black fine-line marking pen

Scissors

Paper trimmer

Computer and printer

Adhesive foam spacers, such as Pop Dots

Ruler; tape

Thick white crafts glue

Glue stick

Here's how

Crop the photos into rectangles, leaving one large enough to fit the purchased mat. Mount the other on black card stock; trim narrow borders. Tape a photo behind the mat. To create a two-color mat, cut a photo mat with wide borders. Cut a strip of card stock to fit the height of the mat. Punch a hole in the two right-hand corners. Glue the color strip to the right edge of the mat. Glue the photo in the mat center. Add eyelets where desired.

1 Use a playful computer letter style to print the letters T, A, and P on white paper. Trim rectangles around the letters. Use a black marking pen to roughly outline each letter, adding dots in the corners. Outline the top, bottom, and right edge of the background page in the same way.

Mount letters on black card stock. Glue the title in place.

2 Glue the black card stock strip along the left edge of the background.

3 Glue the photos on the background. Glue the decorative border die cut over the edge of the black paper strip.

4 Using a computer, print a caption on white paper and mount on colored card stock; trim a narrow border. Use a marking pen to add a dot in each corner. Glue it to the background.

5 Write journaling on white paper. Cut out the journaling. Roughly outline the copy block and add a dot in each corner. Mount on black card stock and trim narrow borders. Glue onto the background. Glue the dance girl die cut to the page with a spacer.

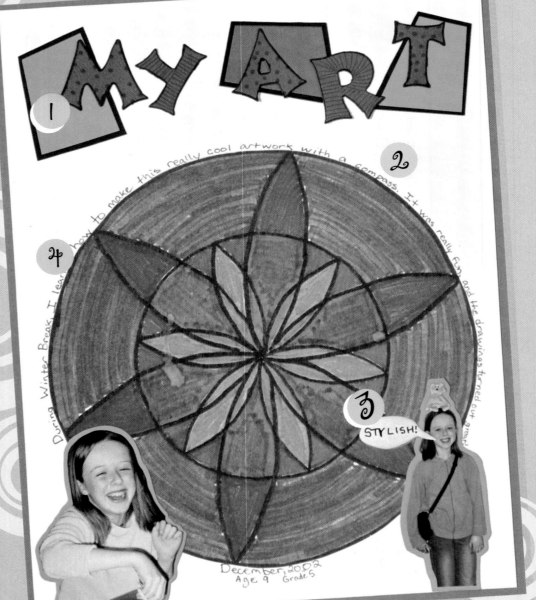

MY ART

During Winter Break, I learned how to make this really cool artwork with a compass. It was really fun and the drawings turned out great!

STYLISH!

December, 2002
Age 9 Grade 5

Keep track of your favorite artwork by putting it in your scrapbook with photos of the artist ... YOU!

What you'll need

Photos of you

8½×11-inch piece of purple card stock

Scraps of card stock in turquoise, purple, black and dark pink (or in colors to match your artwork)

A 8¼×10¾-inch color photocopy of your drawing or painting on white card stock

Scrap of vellum

Marking pens in black and a color to match art

Alphabet punch

Scissors

Glue stick

Here's how

Trim photos around your body shape. Glue the silhouettes to turquoise card stock and trim narrow borders. Center and glue the photocopy of your art on the purple background sheet.

1 Punch the title letters from purple card stock. Use a black marking pen to outline each letter. Decorate each letter by drawing stripes and dots on the letters.

2 Cut three irregular shapes from color card stock. Glue on black card stock and trim narrow borders. Arrange title at top of page and glue in place.

3 Cut a small caption bubble from vellum. Use a black marking pen to write a word or thought on it. Glue the caption and photos on the background.

4 Use a color marking pen to write journaling around edges of artwork.

Here's a tip for you!

If you want an acid-free scrapbook (that will last FOREVER!), have your artwork photocopied on acid-free card stock. Most scrapbooking stores carry acid-free papers, stickers, and trims.

MY DREAM CAR

2

1

'62 On our last day of our Florida vacation, we went to Old Town where there were hundreds of cars. We saw this one and got to ride in the parade with the other. Someday, I'll have one!

When you get to sit in the driver's seat of your dream wheels, be sure to snap a photo to show your friends.

What you'll need

- **8×10-inch photo**
- **12-inch square of turquoise card stock**
- **Two 12-inch squares coordinating patterned papers for background**
- **5¼×3-inch scrap of print paper for journaling mat**
- **White card stock**
- **¼-inch red metallic numeral stickers**
- **1½-inch stickers for title in black and white**
- **Scissors; ruler**
- **Black marking pen**
- **Glue stick**

Here's how

To create the background, cut a 5-inch strip from one background paper and a 6-inch strip from the other. Slant and mount the papers, as shown on page, left, on the card stock. Trim away any paper that hangs over the edge of the card stock. Crop the photo if you wish and mount it onto the background.

1 Create a journal box by gluing white card stock in the center of the remaining print paper. Use stickers to start journaling with a year or anything you wish. Complete the journaling in handwriting.

2 To make the title, arrange and stick on the black letters. Place the white letters over black ones, moving them up and to the right a bit to create the look of a shadow.

Here's a tip for you!

You can make instant shadows by layering light shapes over dark shapes (like the lettering, opposite). Try it with journal boxes, numbers, mats, stickers, etc. You'll find making shadows easy!

Got Cookies?

What you'll need

- Photos; two 8-inch squares of white card stock
- Card stock in green, red, and white
- ¾-inch green alphabet stickers; girl sticker
- Scissors; paper cutter
- Ruler; zigzag border ruler
- Pencil; paper punch
- Black fine-line marking pen; glue stick

Here's how

Crop the photos into rectangles or squares. Cut around a photo. To mat some of the photos, glue to white card stock and trim narrow borders. Mount on red card stock and trim narrow borders.

1 Cut a 3-inch square from red card stock. Cut it in half, corner to corner. Glue

5 Got Cookies?

6 I got to sort and count cookies this year for Girl Scouts. Our troop sold cookies at the Cookie Kick-off at a booth sale. We sold 1060 boxes of cookies!!

1

Girl Scouts love to sell cookies, and these pages reflect a job well done!

each triangle to green card stock and trim borders. Glue one triangle on the right edge of one page, 1 inch from the top. Glue the other triangle to the left edge of the other page, 2 inches from the top.

2 Cut two 1½×8-inch strips from green. Lay the zigzag ruler at the edge of each strip, trace, and cut out.

3 Cut two ¼×8-inch white strips. Glue a strip to each green border, ¼ inch from the straight edge.

4 Punch holes in the points of the green border. Punch circles from red card stock. Glue circles evenly spaced along the white strips. Glue a decorated green strip to the outside edge of each page.

5 Use alphabet stickers to spell out title.

6 Cut a small piece of white card stock, draw rules, and write journaling. Mount on red card stock and trim narrow borders. Glue all pieces to the background.

My Own Room ... at Last!

What you need

Photos

12-inch squares of card stock in bright pink and yellow

Card stock in lime green, purple, turquoise, yellow, bright pink, and black

Acrylic jewels

Black alphabet stickers

Black and silver fine-line marking pens

Paper trimmer; scissors

Decorative-edge scissors

Circle cutter; pencil

Thick white crafts glue

Toothpick; glue stick

Here's how

Crop the photos; using a circle cutter for round cuts. Mount the photos on card stock you like. Trim the borders using straight or decorative-edge scissors. Use the circle

My Own Room

5

4

I have the best parents in the world! For my 12th birthday they surprised me with MY VERY OWN ROOM in the basement. It is soooo COOL!! I love it!

3

Mom says I look like the driver in the painting ☺!

BRITNE

Happiness is ... YOUR OWN ROOM!

Dedicate a bright page or two to your own totally awesome space!

I love my sis...

... even MORE when we don't have to share a room!

friends like to hang out me in my new room!

Mom and Dad had a cool mural painted on my wall. I can't wait to drive!!!

BRIVE

Sage likes my room!

At Last!

cutter to cut background shapes and outlines from turquoise and green card stock. Cut a journal rectangle from black using decorative-edge scissors. Mount on turquoise card stock; trim.

1 Use the pages, left, as a guide, and draw large flower and leaf patterns. Cut out shapes. Trace around the patterns on card stock; cut out.

2 Cut 2½-inch strips from pink and yellow card stock. Tape them together. Glue the strips at the top of each contrasting page.

3 Glue the flowers, journal box, circles, and photos in place. To make something stand out on a photo, use an outline circle.

4 Journal around the photos and circles. Use a silver pen to write on black journal box.

5 Press the title stickers in place.

6 Use crafts glue on a toothpick to glue jewels on flowers.

Milwaukee

What you'll need

Photos and newspaper clippings

Two 12-inch squares of black card stock

Red mulberry paper

Glitter paper in white and red

Alphabet stickers: ¼ inch gold and 1½ inch metallic red; ¼-inch black numerals

Large star punches in long and squatty styles

Templates in circle and oval shapes

Scissors; corner rounder

Fine-line silver marking pen; pencil; glue stick

Here's how

Crop the photos. To create oval or circle shapes, trace around a template on the photo; cut out. Use a corner rounder on straight-cut photos. Mount two photos on white

3

5

January 20

122

Being a gymnast makes you special—be sure and record all the happy moments.

glitter paper and trim narrow borders. Mount one photo on mulberry paper and tear a border around photo.

1 Tear a 2×11-inch strip of mulberry paper. Center strip at bottom of right background about ½ inch from the bottom. Glue down the strip.

2 Punch 5 long stars from white glitter paper and one squatty star. Punch one squatty star from red. Glue long stars on the strip of mulberry paper. Press black numbers on stars to show rankings.

3 Stick letters for title at the bottom of the left background page. Glue photos and newspaper clippings where you like, grouping and overlapping some to become units.

4 Use gold alphabet stickers to add words, such as "BARS," "VAULT," and "BEAM" by mulberry paper. Glue squatty stars where desired.

5 Journal with a silver pen.

More about ME! Titles

When it's "all about you" (some days are like that!) use these happenin' headlines!

Dreaming, I'm just dreaming!

I never thought I could, but...!

LOOK AT ME!

MY FAVORITE PLACE

Hold the applause . . .

Too cool for words!

WOW! Do you believe this?!

Watch THiS!

Take a Bow!

Here I Gooooo ...

PURE FUN!

I Love This!

This is just sooooo ME!

index

sources

Adhesives
Aleenes
duncancrafts.com

Centis
Centis Consumer Products Division
888/236-8476

Elmer's Glue Stick
800/848-9400
elmers.com
comments@elmers.com

Suze Weinberg Design Studio
732/761-2400
732/761-2410 (fax)
Suzenj@aol.com

Tombow USA
800/835-3232
tombowusa.com

Brads
Magic Scraps
972/238-1838
magicscraps.com

Buttons
Le Bouton Buttons
Blumenthal Lansing Co.
563/538-4211
563/538-4243 (fax)
sales@buttonsplus.com

Die Cuts
Cock A Doodle
800/262-9727
cockadoodle.com

Deluxe Cuts
480/497-9005
707/922-2175 (fax)
deluxecuts.com

Fresh Cuts
Rebecca Sower
EK Success Ltd.
eksuccess.com

Griff's Shortcuts
989/894-5916
griffs-shortcuts.com

Little Extras
361/814-9191
littleextrasdiecuts.com

Stamping Station
801/444-3838
stampingstation.com

Eyelets
Persnippity
801/523-3338
persnippity.com

Fiber
Cut-It-Up
530/389-2233
cut-it-up.com

Foam Squares
Therm O Web
800/323-0799

**Opaque Writers/
Waterproof Markers**
EK Success Ltd.
eksuccess.com
(Wholesale only. Available at most
crafts stores.)

Photographic Images
Shotz Photo Papers by Danelle Johnson
Creative Imaginations, Inc.
cigift.com

Press-On Gems
Stampa Rosa, Inc.
707/527-8267
stamparosa.com

Protective Sleeves
Westrim Crafts
888/727-2727

Rubber Stamps/Ink Pads
Art Impressions
800/393-2014
artimpressions.com

Stampin' Up!
801/601-5400
stampinup.com

Scissors, Punches & Rounders
Creative Memories
800/341-5275
creativememories.com

Fiskars Scissors
608/259-1649
fiskars.com

Emagination Crafts, Inc.
866/238-9770
service@emaginationcraftsinc.com

EK Success Ltd.
eksuccess.com
(Wholesale only. Available at most
crafts stores.)

Scrapbook Papers
All My Memories
888/553-1998

Anna Griffin
404/817-8170
404/817-0590 (fax)
annagriffin.com

Art Accents
360/733-8989
artaccents.net

Bazzill Basics Paper
480/558-8557
bazzillbasics.com

Colorbök
800/366-4660
colorbok.com

Daisy D's Paper Co.
801/447-8955
daisydspaper.com

DMD, Inc.
800/805-9890

Doodlebug
801/966-9952

Family Archives
888/622-6556
heritagescrapbooks.com

Frances Meyer, Inc.
800/372-6237
francesmeyer.com

Hot Off The Press, Inc.
800/227-9595
paperpizazz.com

Karen Foster Design, Inc.
Karenfosterdesign.com

Making Memories
800/286-5263
makingmemories.com

Memories Forever
Westrim Crafts
800/727-2727
westrimcrafts.com

The Paper Loft
866/254-1961 (toll free)
paperloft.com
(Wholesale only. Available at most crafts
stores.)

Pixie Press
888/834-2883
pixiepress.com

Plaid Enterprises, Inc.
800/842-4197
plaidonline.com

Provo Craft
provocraft.com
(Wholesale only. Available at most
crafts stores.)

Sandylion
800/387-4215
905/475-0523 (international)
sandylion.com

Scrap-ease What's New, Ltd.
800/272-3874
480/832-2928 (fax)
whatsnewltd.com

Sweetwater
14711 Road 15
Fort Morgan, CO 80701
970/867-4428

Westrim Crafts
800/727-2727

Wübie Prints
wubieprints.com
(Wholesale only. Available at most
crafts stores.)

Two Busy Moms
800/272-4794
TwoBusyMoms.com

Stickers
Canson
800/628-9283
canson-us.com

The Gifted Line
John Grossman, Inc.
310/390-9900

Highsmith
800/558-3899
highsmith.com

K & Co.
816/389-4150
KandCompany.com

me & my BIG ideas
949/589-4607
meandmybigideas.com

Mrs. Grossman's Paper Co.
800/429-4549
mrsgrossmans.com

Once Upon A Scribble
702/896-2181
onceuponascribble.com

Paper Punch
800/397-2737

Paper House Productions
800/255-7316
paperhouseproductions.com

SRM Press
800/323-9589
srmpress.com
(Wholesale only. Available at most crafts
stores.)

Stickopotamus
P.O. Box 1047
Clifton, NJ 07014-1047
973/594-0540 (fax)
stickopotamus.com